Better Business Writing

Steven M. Bragg

AccountingTools®

ISBN 978-1-64221-181-8

For more information about AccountingTools® products, visit our Web site at www.accountingtools.com.

Table of Contents

About the Author

Steven Bragg, CPA, has been the chief financial officer or controller of four companies, as well as a consulting manager at Ernst & Young. He received a master's degree in finance from Bentley College, an MBA from Babson College, and a Bachelor's degree in Economics from the University of Maine. He has been a two-time president of the Colorado Mountain Club, and is an avid alpine skier, mountain biker, and certified master diver. Mr. Bragg resides in Centennial, Colorado. He has written more than 300 books and courses, including *New Controller Guidebook*, *GAAP Guidebook*, and *Payroll Management*. He has also written the *The Auditors* science fiction trilogy.

Steven maintains the accountingtools.com web site, which contains continuing professional education courses, the Accounting Best Practices podcast, and thousands of articles on accounting subjects.

Better Business Writing

Introduction

Clear and persuasive writing is an essential element of modern business, since it allows you to present your case more effectively. This is a skill that anyone can learn. In this book, we cover the essential components of better business writing, with the goal of improving your writing production.

The Case for Better Business Writing

Most people do not spend much time polishing their writing. Instead, they think that throwing together a quick message is a more efficient use of their time, without realizing what the impact of these marginal communications may be on the recipients. One's supervisors, colleagues, and customers will form an opinion based on the quality of the writing they receive. Consequently, sloppy writing will trigger the opinion that the writer does not care about his work, while excellent-quality work tells the recipient the reverse. For example, here are two versions of the same message, where the first version is entirely too verbose; the second version strips the message down to its essentials:

> Example 1: As matters stand with the educators in the accounting departments of the region's universities, it should be reasonable for us to expect that our latest audit recruits should be able to handle the simpler auditing tasks, such as bank reconciliations. But this is not the case. Instead, time and again, our audit managers find that they have to stop what they are doing and repeatedly show new auditors how to deal with this most simple of all auditing tasks.

> Example 2: Given the level of audit training in local colleges, you would think that new auditors would be able to complete a bank reconciliation. However, many audit managers have to train new staff in this baseline technique.

The differences are obvious. The first example is excessively verbose and florid, while the second example is half the length, while conveying the same information. An essential point of the second example is that it gets right to the point; it states the basics and stops.

Those who issue unpolished writing might make the case that doing so saves time, since they do not spend time agonizing over every word. This is not really the case, because a poorly-written missive is not easy for the recipient to understand. When this is the case, the writer may get sucked into a round of clarifications that would not have been necessary if he had spent more time up-front, refining his writing.

A further concern is that a poorly-written communication wastes the time of the recipient, who has to puzzle over it to extract its meaning. If the recipient misunderstands the message, it is quite possible that she will make an incorrect decision, which will eventually cause trouble for the writer. A related concern is that bad writing causes the recipient to overlook an important fact, which may lead to inaction that could also be disastrous for the company.

Poor writing can be a waste of time when the writing is intended for an outside audience, such as when a report is being sent to a client. When this is the case, the writer's supervisor will need to revise the document (usually at the last moment) before it can be issued. This represents a major waste of time for the supervisor, whose time is arguably more valuable than that of the writer. And, when these changes are made at the last minute, it is more likely that the final product will not be as polished as the company would like, resulting in a less positive outcome for the business – such as losing a prospective sale.

A final reason for better business writing is that obvious flaws in a printed product will require the company to throw out the product and try again. As an example, a sales associate of the author took it upon himself to develop a printed brochure for the company, on which he committed the company to pay $5,000 in printing costs. He did not have anyone review his writing. After the brochure was printed, the company president found 13 typos in it, and immediately ordered all copies to be thrown in the trash. In short, there is a real out-of-pocket cost associated with bad writing.

The Mindset

In order to achieve better business writing, the first step is to recognize that you are a professional writer. This is the case when *any* aspect of your job involves writing – even if it encompasses no more than sending emails to other people within the company. As a professional writer, your performance, to some degree, is based on the quality of your writing. Once you have realized that this is the case, it is easier to commit to a program of improving your writing.

The Writing Process

There is a process flow that underlies high-quality writing. Following the steps noted in this section make it much easier to develop high-quality written output. Each step is separately discussed in the following sub-sections.

1. Understand the Purpose

The first step in the writing process is to have a firm understanding of what the final written product is supposed to be about. For example, is the intent to persuade a customer to upgrade to your latest model, or perhaps to gain a person's attendance at the company's trade show booth, or maybe just to have everyone attend a meeting on short notice? Knowing the purpose makes it easier to clearly state the issue and what needs to be accomplished. By keeping the outcome in mind, you can also pare away at early drafts, so that the final product is perfectly targeted at what you want. For example, a collections manager is confronted with yet another overdue receivable for a customer that has persistently paid 40 days late on every invoice sent to it for the past year. It does a significant amount of business with the company. Depending on your desired outcome, the content of the collection email to the customer's payables manager could vary substantially. Consider the following scenarios:

Example 1: [You have met with the payables manager several times and are on good terms with her. The purpose is to be paid, while preserving the relationship.]

Hi Shelly,

I'm sure it's an oversight, but invoice #40762 for $18,210 is not yet paid, and it is a month overdue. Just to be on the safe side, I am sending you a copy of the invoice by overnight mail. Perhaps we can get together for lunch next week to discuss a better process flow for payments?

Example 2: [You have a strained relationship with the payables manager, and the president has approved the termination of this customer if prompt payment cannot be obtained. The purpose is to enforce payment terms.]

Dear Ms. Patterson,

I am contacting you yet again about a late invoice payment, this time for invoice #40762. Every payment for the past year has been at least 40 days late. You appear to have a policy of always paying late, which is not acceptable for us. Therefore, if I do not receive payment from you within two business days, we will no longer accept orders from you for new deliveries. If you *do* pay within two days, then I expect you to observe our net 30 terms on all future invoices. Thank you for your attention to this matter, and please feel free to call me if you want to discuss the matter further.

The tone of the two emails is entirely different. In the first case, the purpose of maintaining relations is clearly evident, while in the second case, the writer has no intention of doing so, and is instead sternly focusing on immediate payment and future compliance with the company's payment terms.

2. Understand the Recipient

Every writing project should be based on a firm understanding of the circumstances of the recipient. Perhaps she is under a great deal of pressure, and so prefers to see one-sentence emails. Or, perhaps she is motivated by getting home at a reasonable hour, and so does not want to see any non-critical messages after 5 p.m. Or, she is under pressure to reduce costs in her department, and so is more likely to read emails that focus on cost reductions. These factors impact how a message should be written. If you write a message that is properly tailored to the recipient, it is much more likely to have an impact on the person. In essence, focus on what is in it for them.

For example, you want to set up a materials review board in the warehouse that tags obsolete inventory for immediate disposal. Members of the review board should (ideally) come from the materials management, engineering, and accounting departments. The managers of each of these departments has different needs, so it makes sense to send a differently-worded request to each manager that focuses on how this proposal will help them. For example:

> Accounting: I would like to form a materials review board that will identify obsolete inventory, so that it can be disposed of. This would reduce the obsolete inventory reserve in the accounting records, and also minimize the amount of auditor review time associated with obsolete inventory. Would you be interested in attending MRB meetings?

> Engineering: I would like to form a materials review board that will identify obsolete inventory, so that it can be disposed of. This would help you spot instances in which bills of material are incorrect, where the company has mistakenly bought more raw materials than it needs. Would you be interested in attending MRB meetings?

> Materials Management: I would like to form a materials review board that will identify obsolete inventory, so that it can be disposed of. By attending, you could keep the group from disposing of raw materials that you are scheduling for future production runs. Would you be interested in attending the meetings?

In each case, the middle sentence is used to provide a recipient-specific reason for attending.

What about cases in which there are many recipients? It is impossible to write a separate message to each one; instead, write it for someone who is not a specialist in your area of expertise. This means wanting to ensure that the recipients, whoever they are, understand what you are trying to tell them. This involves replacing jargon and complex concepts with the simplest possible explanations. For example, the following turgid text might (unwisely) be used when explaining a company's financial results to its employees:

> We generated a net profit percentage of 7.2% in the last quarter, which was driven by a change in sales mix in the southeast region, a positive purchasing variance in the materials management department, and reduced shrinkage losses in the production area. In addition, we used foreign exchange hedging to offset losses in our payments to foreign suppliers.

While the preceding text might be perfectly understandable to a trained accountant, it sounds like a foreign language to someone from any other department. Instead, the text could be restated as follows, to make it more understandable to a mixed-experience audience.

> We earned $390,000 in the last three months. We did it by selling more expensive products in the southeast region, saving money on raw material purchases, and maintaining better control over the inventory. We also used some financial strategies to minimize our payments to foreign suppliers.

The latter approach eliminates all mention of profit percentages, sales mix, shrinkage, and hedging, while still highlighting the reasons for the profit in way that most people can understand.

3. Collect Material

The preceding two steps provide the general framework within which the work of writing can now begin. The first step in the actual writing phase is to collect material, such as source documents and ideas. This material can come from a variety of sources, including the following:

- Books
- Conversations with others
- Internet articles
- Magazine article clippings
- Personal ideas
- Personal observations

When the writing project is a small one and there are few source materials, it is reasonable to stop here, with a small unconsolidated pile of paper, and proceed to the next step. However, if the project is more substantial, with a correspondingly large amount of material, some additional organizing is advised. In the latter case, consider itemizing everything in a spreadsheet, noting the general idea of each source document, the reference number of the document[1], and its source. A sample entry in the spreadsheet appears in the following exhibit.

Materials Summarization

Idea	Reference Number	Source
Cod stocks are plunging worldwide	M-12	*Fisheries International*, May 20X3 edition, pg. 57

In the preceding exhibit, the reference "M-12" reference number means that this is the 12th article within the magazines ("M") source category.

As references are used within your written product, format the related reference in the spreadsheet with a strikethrough (like ~~this~~), to indicate that the reference has been used. Doing so effectively highlights anything that has not yet been used.

Logging everything into a spreadsheet can seem like a lot of pointless additional work, but when there are many source documents, having a reference spreadsheet can be central to the task of organizing the project.

4. Create an Outline

Based on the preceding steps, create a few sentences that contain the main points you want to convey. Think through the supporting logic as thoroughly as possible, since the resulting document will reflect your thinking – and clear logic results in a more forceful document. Then arrange these sentences in the most logical order, so that the first point flows into the second point, and so on. Once these points have been listed, insert bullet points below each one that reinforce the point being conveyed. It is likely

---

[1] If a reference number is to be used, then an additional step is to go through the pile of supporting materials and prominently mark each one with the applicable reference number.

that these points will need to be reshuffled somewhat, so block out time to review the list.

The reverse of this approach is to mentally organize the project while writing it, which is likely to result in a muddled final product. If so, you will end up reviewing your completed text, decide that it makes no sense, and start over again – which is not a good use of your time.

EXAMPLE

The president of Mule Corporation, maker of "Bad Ass" motorcycles, is interested in developing an electric motorcycle. He asks Benjamin Balky, the marketing director, to write a memo that discusses the main marketing issues associated with selling such a machine. Mr. Balky arrives at the following outline of key points to be made:

1. Traditional buyers will not buy an electric motorcycle.

    o   They want the throaty rumble of the existing model's gas-powered engine.
    o   Without that noise, there will be no macho association with the company's products.

2. The company needs to address a more environmentally-conscious group of buyers.

    o   These buyers will be attracted to the use of electricity to power the motorcycle.
    o   Addressing these new buyers will require different marketing, since all current marketing is targeted at a macho group of buyers.

3. Doing so could increase overall sales.

    o   With separate marketing campaigns, the company should be able to retain its existing customers while attracting an entirely new set of customers.
    o   With an expanded customer base, overall sales should increase.

Mr. Balky's points clearly state a case for marketing the electric motorcycle to an entirely new group of buyers, rather than trying to sell it to the company's traditional customer base.

---

5. Write

With the outline in hand, write the text as quickly as possible, all the way through to the end. There will be time for extensive polishing in the next step, so don't worry about writing exemplary text at this point. Otherwise, if you stop to work in detail on each sentence, there is a good chance that writer's block will set in, which can greatly delay completion of the project.

A useful way to blow through the first draft is to set a difficult completion target, such as writing 4,000 words in one day, or writing about the first discussion point within the next hour. When speed-writing in this manner, avoid all editing, which takes a great deal of time. Instead, push straight through to the end, using the outline as your guide. The reason for taking this approach is that the act of writing is creative, while the act of editing is very nearly the reverse. Since these tasks are so different, they are inherently incompatible, and so must be separated.

If there is any point at which you get stuck in the writing process, just skip ahead to the next topic and keep writing. By doing so, you are staying in creative mode, rather than dropping into the painful drudgery of writer's block. Once the next topic is complete, circle around to the incomplete part and see if you are now able to continue with the work. If not, move to yet another topic and return to the incomplete part at a later date for another try – and so on.

> **Tip:** When you are suffering from writer's block, start anywhere in the text at all – wherever you think you have something to say, then begin there. You can fill in the rest later.

6. Revise

With the first pass complete, it is time to work back through the text and decide whether what you've written is what you intended, as stated in the outline. If not, this is a good time to rethink how the document should read, which may call for extensive restatements of the text. As part of the revision process, consider the following points:

- How clearly have I stated my foundational points?
- Is there any missing logic?
- Are there any false or unsupported statements?
- Is the writing politically correct in terms of the likely readers?
- Do my closing statements accurately reflect what was said in the document?

> **Tip:** If there is time available to do so, insert a break of several days between writing the first draft and revising it. Doing so breaks your initial association with the writing, so that you can more dispassionately review it and make better changes.

EXAMPLE

Maeve Wilson has been asked to write a memo to the employees of Thundering Herd Consulting, telling them about a change in the accounting department's expense reporting procedure. She begins with the following first draft:

> We are instituting a new expense reporting procedure. When you have a reimbursement request, login to the company website and click on the "Expense Report" procedure. Then enter your employee ID number, the dates and amounts of all expenditures made, and upload a photo of each related receipt.

After reading the first draft, Ms. Wilson realizes that she has said nothing about why these changes are being made, or how they will benefit employees. Instead, she has simply conveyed the basic points of an expense reporting procedure. These additional points are included in the following second draft:

> The accounting department has been reimbursing employees, on average, within four days of the receipt of expense reports, with some reimbursements taking as long as

10 days. In order to make payments more quickly, we are instituting a new procedure, which is as follows:

Login to the company website and click on the "Expense Report" procedure. Then enter your employee ID number, the dates and amounts of all expenditures made, and upload a photo of each related receipt. We will take it from there.

This new procedure allows you to submit expense reports 24/7, even when you are on the road. We expect to issue reimbursement payments within one business day, so that your personal cash flows will not be impacted when traveling on company business.

The second draft clearly states the reason why the changes are being made, and goes on to identify the improvement in payments to employees. This revised form of the memo should greatly improve employee acceptance of the new procedure.

---

7. Edit

Once you are satisfied with the concepts stated in the text, it is time to think through such matters as word choices, excessive verbiage, transitions from one concept to the next, and so forth. When writing a book, the author makes at least ten passes through the document, each time looking for something different that needs fixing, such as:

- Are the chapter numbers correct?
- Are the page headers in each chapter correct?
- Are the section headers sufficiently informative?
- Are there any formatting errors in tables?
- Are there any typographical errors?
- Do all tables have headers?
- Have all passive tense sentences been eliminated?
- Have all tables been referenced in the text?
- Is the font size consistently applied?
- Is the page numbering correct?
- Is there a summary section at the end of each chapter?
- Is there a way to reduce the verbiage?
- Is there proper spacing between bullet points?

It is impossible to take care of these tasks in a single pass through the document, since many items will inevitably not be corrected – so don't try. It is more time-consuming, but much more accurate, to make multiple reviewing passes through the document.

> **Note:** The evaluation phase may require as much time as all of the preceding steps combined.

Parting Thoughts

The writing process described in this section should be followed as described. However, it is also iterative, since there will be cases in which additional material arrives near the end of the process and needs to be incorporated into the writing. During the evaluation process, you may decide to throw out some (or all) of the writing and start over and try writing it in a different way. Consequently, expect to loop through some aspects of this sequence before completing a writing project.

The Opening, Middle, and Close

In a business document of any length, there should be an opening statement that summarizes what the document is about, a middle section that expands upon the opening statement, and a closing section that summarizes the main concepts in the document.

A good opening statement tells the reader the main point of the document. If the reader wanted to, she could skip the rest of the document, though doing so would deprive her of any supporting points and arguments.

A sample opening that covers the essentials of an entire document is as follows:

> We are in the process of replacing our accounting software with a new package. BoringSoft is one of the replacement candidates. The review committee charged with examining the finalist software packages recommends that we reject the BoringSoft product, for the following reasons:
>
> - The software does not have an automated cloud backup feature, which we believe is necessary, given the flood damage to our server room last year.
> - The software does not offer a currency hedge accounting feature, which we expect will become more necessary when we begin selling in Europe next year.
> - We have heard from six other users of the software that BoringSoft's customer service is substandard, specifically in regard to their knowledge of problems and work-arounds in the receivables and payables modules.

This example covers the essentials – a recommendation not to buy the software, and the specific reasons for this recommendation. If readers want to proceed into the details of exactly what the six other users of BoringSoft's software had to say about its customer support problems, then they can proceed to the middle section of the document. If not, the opening statement is sufficient for their needs.

> **Tip:** There is no requirement to keep the opening section down to a spartan minimum. Instead, write what needs to be said, and stop. If that is one sentence, then fine. If it requires a full page, then that is fine, too.

The middle section of the document contains your supporting points. The main issue here is deciding upon the best order in which to state them. The best arrangement is the one that is the most persuasive and memorable for the reader. Consider the following possibilities:

- *Categorization.* Sometimes a simple list is sufficient. For example, the attractive features of a new company location could be listed, ranging from low property taxes to adjacent schools.
- *Cause and effect.* State a situation and its logical outcome. For example, show how investing in machines of different production capacity will alter the revenue level of the company.
- *Order of importance.* List the most important item first, with lesser items stated lower down in the report. For example, note that the most important cause of customer satisfaction is product ease of use, followed by seven other reasons in declining order.
- *Pros and cons.* It can be useful to present both sides of an argument, to give the appearance of having given a balanced decision. For example, show how an investment in equipment will improve product quality, but at an increased cost per unit.
- *Time series.* Create a chronological list when you want to state a sequence of events, such as when outlining what happened that caused a production failure to occur.

The document close is either a call to action or a summarization of the information that was conveyed in the report. It should be brief and forceful, rather than meandering to a piddling end. For example:

> In short, we believe that the acquisition of the Seaside Business Park is an excellent investment, due to its low maintenance costs and property taxes – and, of course, because the seller is motivated to sell right now. His offer is open until next Tuesday, and I urge you to accept it. Thank you!

Types of Sentences

Better business writing involves the use of multiple types of sentences. You should liberally mix these sentence types into any business document, to make it more interesting. The various sentence structures are as follows:

- *Head-on sentence.* In this sentence, the main point appears first, followed by other clauses that expand upon or support it. This is the most common sentence used in business writing, since it gets straight to the point. For example, "We should buy the new helicopter for next fire season, or else we will not be able to respond quickly to reported fires."
- *Build-up sentence.* This sentence is designed to make the reader wait until the end for the main idea. The intent, as the name implies, is to build up reader interest, pulling the person through to the very end. For example, "Assuming that you can overcome the leasing problem and the delayed liquor license, I support your restaurant opening date."

- *Rhetorical question*. This sentence asks a question and then answers it. The intent is to focus the reader's attention on a specific issue. For example: "Why are our sales down? Because we close our stores two hours before anyone else, so the neighboring stores scoop up our customers!"
- *Interrupted sentence*. A comment is inserted into the middle of a sentence in order to call attention to a specific point. These comments can insert an excessive degree of choppiness into a document, so use them sparingly. An example is, "These profits – if you can call them that – are barely above the breakeven point."
- *Parallel sentence*. This sentence contains a series of similar phrases to give it a rhythmic flow. It can be used to drive home a key point. For example, "These groundwater problems are of concern to our families, our community, and our way of life!"
- *Fragmentary sentence*. This is an incomplete sentence that can be used occasionally to liven up a multi-sentence statement. For example, "What would we give to land the Bartley account? A lot!"

The head-on sentence is the mainstay of business writing, but it can be overused. Accordingly, mix up the message with the other sentence types noted here, to gain the attention of the reader.

Proper Paragraph Structure

A paragraph is a distinct section of a piece of writing, usually dealing with a single theme and indicated by a new indentation or line. It is designed to fulfill several functions. One is to develop a theme, which appears in the first sentence and is expanded upon in subsequent sentences. It also provides a logical break in the material, so that the reader moves from one theme to the next. And finally, it creates a visual break on the page, signaling the start of a new topic.

The topic sentence states the main idea of the paragraph, while the rest of the paragraph supports and develops the theme with additional details. The topic sentence should be sufficiently well-described that a reader could learn the essentials of a document simply by reading the first sentence of each paragraph. For example:

The cost of training new accounting staff is high. They rarely have expertise in our accounting system, and so need to be sent to the software developer's facility for a week of training. In addition, they require hands-on training in the procedures associated with the functions to which they have been assigned. Finally, the more senior staff have to spend time training them, which represents a high opportunity cost for the company.

In some cases, it can make sense to lead up to the topic sentence, which is therefore placed at the end of a paragraph. For example:

> We are currently spending $400,000 on being a publicly-held business. In addition, our senior management team spent a total of 1,200 hours on the road last year, meeting with investors. Further, the accounting department has had to install 42 new controls to be in compliance with the requirements of Sarbanes-Oxley, and wastes time at the end of each quarter, undergoing a review by our auditors. <u>In short, being a public company is a substantial burden on the business.</u>

A paragraph should be sufficiently long to provide adequate coverage of its theme. The risk in paragraph development is in writing too little or too much. A minimal paragraph has not provided sufficient support for the theme, so that the reader is at risk of being unconvinced. Conversely, an excessively long paragraph exhausts the reader, who may skip through it and not absorb the main points. As a general rule, a paragraph should contain four or five sentences.

Shave Away Excess Words

Remember when writing assignments in school mandated a certain number of words, such as a 2,000-word essay on the differences between Hemingway and Faulkner? The reverse is true in business writing, where you are rewarded for stating your case within the shortest possible number of words. Here are several options for doing so:

- *Drop leading "it" phrases.* A stilted form of writing is to begin a sentence with "It," such as "It should be noted that…" or "It has come to my attention that…" You can usually strike out these words entirely and begin with the next part of the sentence. For example, "~~It should be noted that~~ power usage in the city increases as of sunset."
- *Drop other sentence starters.* Many throwaway words are stuck onto the beginning of sentences. For example, "As per our discussion yesterday," "Attached please find," and "Please be advised" can be stripped from sentences.
- *Drop references to yourself.* Business writing should be about the reader, not the writer, so eliminate as many references to "I" as possible (though some may still be needed). For example, replace "I want to conduct a physical inventory count" with "We need to conduct a physical inventory count." The latter example implies that we are all in this together, which is more likely to gain the approval of the reader.
- *Drop who, which, and that.* The words "who," "which," and "that" can usually be stripped out of a sentence without causing any damage. For example, "Martha Jones, ~~who is~~ the company president, presided at the meeting." Or, "The dunning letter, ~~which is~~ used to prod customers into paying, is a key element of our collections campaign." And finally, "We are developing a procedure ~~that is~~ sufficiently detailed for new hires to follow."
- *Drop weak verbs.* Some verbs get stuffed into a sentence without impacting it. For example, "The vice president will make a decision next Tuesday" could

be pared down by swapping out "make" for "decide," so that the sentence is shortened to read, "The vice president will decide next Tuesday." Or, "The boss came to the conclusion that we needed to lease the next copier" could be replaced by "The boss concluded that we needed to lease the next copier."

- *Drop excess verbs.* One verb per sentence is usually enough. If there are more verbs, consider yanking them out. For example, "The maintenance department can handle the extra refurbishment tasks that you are adding" can be replaced by "We can handle your additional refurbishment tasks."

- *Drop boring intensifiers.* Some words, such as *rather, somewhat, fairly, basically*, and *mostly* do little to intensify the words to which they are attached. Thus, the sentence "Ralph was ~~mostly~~ successful in recording the podcast episode." If a word needs an intensifier, consider replacing it with a more vigorous term. For example, replace *very happy* with *ecstatic*, and replace *very surprised* with *amazed*.

- *Drop prepositions.* A preposition is a word governing and usually preceding a noun or pronoun, and expressing a relation to another word, such as *at, on, with, over*, and *under*. Look for prepositions that can be removed. For example, replace "We have received your donation in the amount of $500" with "We have received your check for $500."

- *Drop foreign phrases.* Some foreign phrases have found their way into the English language, but are not commonly understood. When this the case, replace them with more common English words. Several of these foreign phrases appear in the following exhibit.

Foreign Phrases to Replace

Foreign Phrase	Translation
Bona fide	Genuine
Carte blanche	Full authority
Fait accompli	A done deed
Faux pas	A mistake
Modus operandi	Method
Non sequitur	Not logical
Raison d'etre	Primary reason
Sine qua non	Essential

- *Drop redundancies.* There are many word pairings that essentially say the same thing, such as "alternate choices" and "climb up". In these cases, you can usually strip out a word. The following exhibit contains additional examples of redundancies.

Sample Redundancies

Absolutely complete	Both alike	Each and every	Past experience
Actual fact	Close proximity	Free gift	Repeat again
Adequate enough	Circle around	New innovation	Revert back
Alternate choices	Collaborate together	One and the same	Summarize briefly

Tips for Better Business Writing

In addition to the preceding discussion of the writing process, we include in the following sub-sections a number of pointers for how to improve your business writing further.

Use Supporting Detail

It is quite easy to lose your audience when you make statements without any supporting detail. When this happens, they assume you are a blowhard who likes to rattle off unsubstantiated opinions, and so will ignore you. Instead, provide enough supporting detail to convince the reader. For example, the following sentence is unsubstantiated:

> Arbuckle Industries is never going to pay us for that invoice, so we should sue them right now.

A better approach would have been to provide a sufficient amount of substantiation to bolster the claim, such as:

> Arbuckle has been at least 20 days past due in paying us for the past year. In addition, we had to threaten legal action in order to get paid the last two times. And furthermore, their payables manager said that they just had to go to the bank to extend their loan payments. Therefore, I think Arbuckle Industries is never going to pay us for that invoice; we should sue them right now to obtain payment.

The latter approach gives you credibility with readers, because it shows a solid command of the facts. This approach works when dealing with customers – rather than stating what a great product you have, prove it to them with facts, such as the following:

> Monique Ponto watches hold their value better than any other high-end women's watch. For the last 10 years, our watches have maintained at least 92% resale value, as opposed to no better than an 85% resale value for our closest competitor.

Use Graphics

The prudent use of graphics can greatly increase reader understanding of a document, or at least break up a long span of text. When using graphics, follow these points:

- Include a title for the graphic.
- Position the graphic as close to the related text in the document as possible.
- Refer to the graphic in the text.
- Employ graphics legends that are easy to understand.
- Mix up the types of graphics employed, to make them more distinctive.

A sample graphic that could be included in a discussion of a company's sales funnel appears in the following exhibit. It could be used to drive home the point that the company needs to work on revising its selling process to make it more effective. A graph is useful for assisting readers in understanding trends, proportions, and comparisons.

Sales Funnel Activity as of March 31

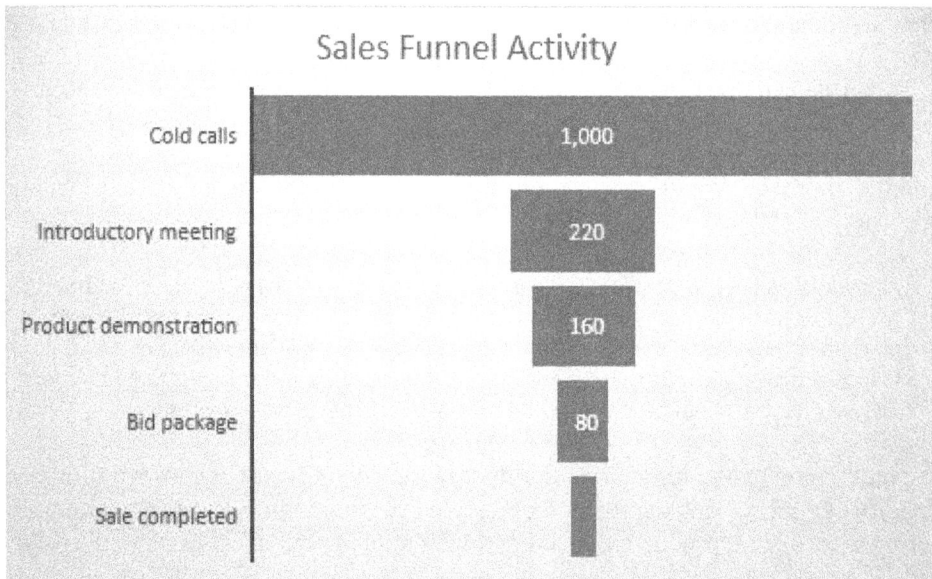

Sales Funnel Activity

Cold calls	1,000
Introductory meeting	220
Product demonstration	160
Bid package	80
Sale completed	

A common graphics option in business writing is a table such as the one in the following exhibit, where the reader needs to have exact figures available, rather than trying to tease them out of a long paragraph.

Late Customer Deliveries (more than two days late)

	June	July	August	September
Akron warehouse	2%	4%	3%	10%
Boston warehouse	1%	2%	1%	3%
Charleston warehouse	14%	10%	8%	6%
Denver warehouse	4%	0%	2%	9%

There may be instances in which a process flow is sufficiently complicated to call for the insertion of a flowchart, just to clarify matters. An example appears in the following exhibit.

Sample Process Flow for Statements of Account

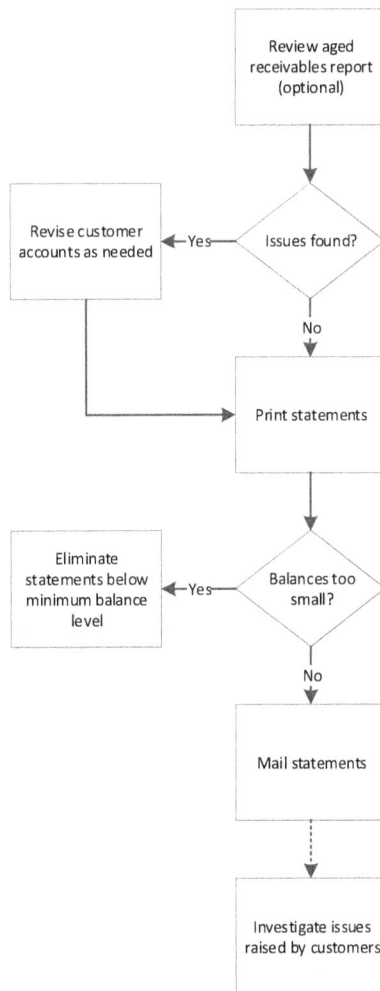

Use the Simplest Words and Sentences

It is easier to convey a message with the simplest possible words. Otherwise, the reader gets bogged down in working out what the words mean. For example, the statement "you prevaricate!" may have no effect at all, while a shorter form of the same statement, such as "you lie!" would probably have a more immediate effect. Similarly, use the smallest possible number of words by stripping out anything that does not improve reader comprehension. For example, the statement "on October 14th" could be replaced by "yesterday," while "as a result" could be replaced by "therefore" or "thus".

Sentences are more readable when they are short. The reader tends to get lost or lose interest when a sentence drags on for an interminable period of time. For example, the following exhibit contains two variations on the same topic, one of which has a much shorter word count that makes it more understandable.

Comparative Writing Lengths

Verbose Writing	Spartan Writing
I am writing to inform you that we did not receive your request for a product return authorization until 100 business days had passed, which exceeded our warranty authorization period by 90 days. Given this unfortunate state of affairs, I am unable to issue you a return authorization at this time. [51 words]	Hi, I'm afraid we received your return request 10 days too late, so I cannot issue you a return authorization. [20 words]

Tip: Simplicity is great, but be mindful of cutting so deep that your writing sounds curt. Always strive for writing that maintains a civil tone.

Explain Terms Separately

When it's absolutely necessary to include a specialized term in your writing, don't jam it into the sentence where the reader first sees it. Doing so results in a long, meandering sentence. Instead, shift the explanation to a separate paragraph, a footnote, or the glossary. For example, a reader of the following sentence about inventory reserves would likely get a headache before completing the sentence:

Because of the amount of obsolete inventory encountered, we plan to set up a reserve for obsolete inventory contra account, which is used to offset the inventory account with which it is paired, so that we can charge obsolete inventory to expense in the current period, rather than later on when specific obsolete inventory items are identified.

A better approach is to break out the description of a contra account from that inordinately long sentence, such as:

> We plan to set up a reserve for obsolete inventory, which is a contra account. A contra account is used to offset the inventory account with which it is paired. By doing so, we can charge obsolete inventory to expense in the current period, rather than recognizing it later, when we identify specific items as being obsolete.

By breaking out the contra account definition, we achieve a shorter sentence structure that is much easier to understand.

Avoid Business Jargon

Always view your writing from the perspective of the reader. If he or she will not understand the jargon in your document, then replace it with simpler text that anyone can understand. This is especially critical when even the more generic business terminology creeps into your writing, such as "mission critical," "outside the box thinking," and "paradigm shift." Having to sort through these buzz words is painfully slow, so do not inflict them on readers. This is a particular concern for accountants, who routinely use so many acronyms that they appear to be speaking in a foreign language. Many examples of business jargon appear in the following table.

Business Jargon and Translations

Business Jargon	Commentary	Simpler Wording
800 pound gorilla	There is a large hairy animal nearby	A force to be reckoned with
Actionable	Something might or might not happen	Something is practical or useful
Action item	More verbose than an action	An action or step
ASAP	Implies that you are in panic mode	Just state a due date
At the end of the day	Seems to refer to 5 p.m.	Therefore
Back of the envelope	Where the stamp goes	A rough note
Balls in the air	Sounds like a juggling act	You are busy
Bells and whistles	Perhaps refers to the components of a train?	Unnecessary features
Best of breed	Sounds like a horse auction	The best
Bang for the buck	Only found on a used car lot	High value for the amount paid
Bleeding edge	Did someone get nicked while shaving?	New approach
Bricks and mortar	Refers to a construction site?	Physical locations
Bring our A game	Time to switch from AAA to major league ball	Do our best
Bring to the table	Refer to a potluck dinner?	What was contributed
Buy-in	Sounds like someone is going gambling	To gain support

Business Jargon	Commentary	Simpler Wording
Change agent	The person makes change at the carnival?	Someone who can make a difference
Circle back	The bank robber is circling around the posse?	Discuss later
Come to Jesus	A deeply religious experience	It's time we had a talk
Deep dive	Better bring an extra tank of air	Thorough analysis
Drill down	Looking for oil	Look at in detail
Drop dead date	The end of the world	Due date
Ducks in a row	Follow Mom to the pond	We are organized
Execute	The French revolution; The Tower of London	We'll do it
Game changer	Sounds like an interception at the goal line	A fundamental change
Give 110%	Mathematically improbable	We commit to it
Granular	A cup of sugar	We'll look at it in detail
Herding cats	Sounds like a small Western movie	Could be management issues
Key takeaways	How much we stole	The key points
Knowledge transfer	Something involving a dumpster	Teach
Laser focus	A cat staring at a red dot	Focus
Level playing field	A football field constructed by a surveyor	Fair competition
Low-hanging fruit	An apple	Easily achievable options
Magic bullet	Immediate large-caliber solution	A cure-all
Mission critical	Military adventurism	Important
Offline	The systems are down!	Speak privately
On the same page	Singing from the same sheet music	We agree
Outside the box	Toys still need to be put away	Creative thinking
Paradigm shift	Star Trek movie	Major change
Push the envelope	A low-grade exercise routine	Expand the boundaries
Radio silent	Better buy a new radio	They have stopped communicating
Sacred cow	A religious view held in India	We cannot change it
Secret sauce	An advanced barbecuing concept	Unique advantage
Seismic shift	A building shifted off its foundations	Major change
Sense of urgency	Trying to look urgent, but not really	Working extra hours
State of the art	The art is apparently being restored	The latest model
Take to the next level	Appears to involve a video game	We are improving
Throw under the bus	A painful form of murder	Betray an ally
Touch base	Appears to involve a game of tag	Reach out
Unpack	The vacation trip is over	Examine in detail

If the previous list seems long, it is not. There are hundreds of other business terms out there, so be wary of including one. When you are deeply immersed in a company's operations, it is all too easy to fall into this mode of speaking, and not even notice that you are doing it.

Avoid Boilerplate Phrases

There is a tendency to stuff boilerplate phrases into business writing. This is a sign that you do not believe your documents are important, and so are giving them reduced attention. Instead, write each missive individually, avoiding all stock phrases. The following exhibit contains a number of boilerplate phrases, along with alternative text.

Boilerplate Phrases and Alternative Text

Boilerplate Phrase	Alternative Text
As per our earlier phone discussion	As we discussed earlier
At your earliest convenience	As soon as possible
Please be advised that	[can be eliminated entirely]
Please do not hesitate to call me if there are any issues	If you have concerns, please call me
Pursuant to your instructions	As you asked
Thank you for your cooperation in regard to this matter	Thank you
We are in receipt of	We have received

Avoid Pretentious Words

Some words appear stuffy and pretentious, so look for shorter words that say the same thing. For example, say "we agreed to" instead of "we acceded to." And why *acquire* something when you can get it? Further, why *ascertain* something when you could simply find out? Similarly, one might try, rather than *endeavoring*, or perhaps rush something through, rather than *expediting* it. A personal favorite pretentious word, since I am in the accounting profession, is to *remunerate* someone, rather than just paying them.

Be Precise

Write so that your output cannot be misunderstood. For example, "Please get me that quote within the next couple of days" can be misunderstood as anywhere from two or even four or five days, which may or may not include weekend days. And what does "We had a great meeting" mean? Did they serve free drinks, or perhaps hand out gift cards, or maybe some decisions were reached? Here are several examples of more precise writing:

We served 1,210 meals to the homeless on Thanksgiving Day.

We will ship your entire order on Tuesday the 10th of July.

During the meeting, we agree to extend the contract for an additional year, to October 31, 20X3.

Avoid Clichés

A cliché is a phrase that is overused and betrays a lack of original thought. They can clutter up a document that might otherwise be clear and to the point. There are hundreds of clichés out there, of which the ones in the following exhibit represent a reasonable sample. Whenever you spot a cliché, find an alternative (and more original) way to say the same thing.

Sample Clichés

Add insult to injury	Diamond in the rough	Hammer it out	Narrow escape
Agree to disagree	Eminently successful	In no uncertain terms	Needs no introduction
All things considered	Equal to the occasion	In this day and age	Other things being equal
As a matter of fact	Exception to the rule	It goes without saying	Pay the piper
At the end of the day	Finishing touches	Keep options open	Piece of cake
Better late than never	Food for thought	Leave no stone unturned	Rise to the occasion
Checkered career	Get our ducks in a row	Lesson for us all	Selling like hotcakes
Crying need	Grave concern	Moment of truth	Wave of the future

If you can't think of alternative wording for a cliché, then at least try to reword it into something original. For example, change "selling like hotcakes" to "selling like iPhones."

Use a Beginning-to-End Chronology

There is a tendency in business writing to only discuss an update to a situation, rather than laying out the entire situation from beginning to end. Doing so makes it difficult for the recipient to understand, especially when he or she is only peripherally involved in the topic under discussion. This type of writing occurs when you are so deeply involved in a project that you don't take the time to view the situation from the perspective of anyone else. This type of writing appears in the left column of the following exhibit, with a more expansive version appearing to its right. In the latter case, we are giving the reader a more complete view of the situation, on order to increase her level of understanding.

Examples of Non-Chronological and Chronological Writing

Non-Chronological Version	Chronological Version
Emerson,	Emerson,
I'm still working on the folks at Ameri-Swipe. They signed the NDA, so I sent them the confidential materials, but then it took four days to receive any kind of a response, and all they would say is that the CFO is still considering her options, and probably won't be able to reach a decision until after the holidays. I'm still working on a direct contact with their CEO, which might be possible if I can corral him into a round of golf – still trying to get past his executive assistant on that one.	As you may recall, Ameri-Life expressed an initial interest in buying our spinoff of the life insurance division. I sent them the briefing materials after receiving an NDA, but their CFO will probably not send us a response until after the holidays. I'm working on setting up a meeting with their CEO to discuss the benefits of why they should buy the division. Can we talk about this sometime next week?
Palmer	Palmer

In the preceding exhibit, the non-chronological version assumes that the reader already knows the baseline subject matter, which may not be the case at all. The chronological version corrects this problem by beginning with a brief discussion of the circumstances, and then proceeds to more current events.

Chronological writing is most useful when dealing with employee evaluations, since the discussions around these events can be emotional. Frequently, the employee will challenge your view of what happened, so it is essential to write down a clear sequence of events and then write the document based on that chronology. For example:

> Mary, last Tuesday, I noticed that you showed up late for work, at 9 a.m. instead of 8 a.m. Then it happened again on Thursday, when you arrived at 9:30 a.m. And today, you showed up at 9:45 a.m. Let's schedule a meeting for this afternoon about why you've been coming in so late...

In the preceding example, the whole premise of the email was based on the chronological order in which the recipient of the message was arriving for work. Without this chronology, Mary might have had grounds to argue the point. For example, the following message, which lacks a chronology, leaves lots of room for whether Mary has been late at all:

> Mary, it appears that you've been late for work several times in the past week. I have not been able to find you in the office until 9 or 10 a.m. on multiple occasions. Let's schedule a meeting for this afternoon about why you've been coming in so late...

Connect the Dots

Or, more specifically, connect the paragraphs. The best business writing neatly connects the thoughts in a string of paragraphs so that they present a logical flow that advances your purpose. Some writers can fit these connecting statements into their writing on the fly, but many choose to instead focus on connecting statements as a separate step during the review process. In the latter case, the result may be some reshuffling of paragraphs, as you realize that the logical flow could be improved by doing so.

The same writing process can be applied to the individual sentences within a paragraph. By doing so, you can guide the reader through a series of arguments or points, as noted in the following paragraph (italics added):

> I think we should reduce the credit limit for H.G. Wells Enterprises, for several reasons. *First*, there has been a change in ownership, and we have not received financial statements from the new owners. *Second*, they started paying us 15 days later as soon as the new owners took over. *And third*, they have started to ramp up their product returns, which have doubled in the past month. *Therefore*, I suggest that we reduce their credit limit from $60,000 to $30,000.

In the following table, we highlight a number of key words that can be used to connect the dots and establish a logical flow.

Key Words to Connect the Dots

Make Connections Based on:	Applicable Connecting Words
Time	Before, after, next, afterward, initially, later, now, then, finally
Location	At the front, in back, along the side, in the center
Add a point	Furthermore, also, in addition, moreover
Concede a point	Admittedly, although, even though, granted, whereas, still
Provide a reason	Thus, it follows that, because, hence, therefore, consequently

Break it up with Sub-Headers

When confronted with a massive slab of text, a reader might be tempted to skip over or skim it. To keep this from happening, insert a few sub-headers that identify the nature of small blocks of text. This approach is also useful for directing people toward the specific elements of a document that they need right now.

When using sub-headers, try to make them as consistent as possible, so that the document as a whole looks more coherent. For example, the sub-headings for a document that discusses visiting Santa at the North Pole might be:

The Walking Route

The Dogsledding Route

The Airplane and Parachuting Route

Denote Trademarks

When your company has a trademarked product, be sure to identify it as such in your correspondence. Without this ongoing identification, the product could legally lose its trademark. Therefore, someone writing about a Pepsi-Cola product would write it as "Pepsi-Cola®". The trademark symbol should be included the first time you write a product name on a page.

Eliminate Gender Bias

The historical default reference in business writing is to say that "he" did this or that. To eliminate gender bias, it is always possible to simply insert "his or her" into a sentence, such as "Each employee will complete his or her assessment, after which we will meet to go over annual performance reviews." However, this is a kludgy approach. Instead, consider replacing the masculine pronoun with *one* or *you*, or using one of the workarounds shown in the following exhibit.

Gender Bias Elimination

Gender-Biased Approach	No Gender Bias
Everyone should submit his expense report.	Everyone should submit an expense report.
An employee can contact his union representative.	You can contact your union representative.
If he works overtime, a supervisor can expect promotion.	A supervisor who works overtime can expect promotion.
If any employee on the production line is concerned about quality, he can shut down the line.	Any production employee who spots a quality problem can shut down the production line.

Use a Reviewer

If there is time available, ask someone not associated with your writing project to read your work. Since these people have no direct association with your work, they are probably similar to your target audience. If your reviewers cannot easily describe the main points in your document or they misunderstand what you are saying, then it is time for a revision. Ideally, the basic concepts you are trying to convey should leap off the page.

In addition to a general review, ask for more detailed analyses, covering such topics as:

- Are there grammar issues?
- Should additional information have been conveyed?
- Is there a way to shorten the amount of text?
- Can the tone be improved?

> **Tip:** Always accept revision suggestions cheerfully; if you get defensive, your reviewers will stop making suggestions.

It can be useful to use the same reviewers on a recurring basis. These people will begin to understand the areas in which you tend to have issues, and so can spotlight them more readily in the future. Also, their writing skills might improve as a result of these ongoing discussions.

When you are the only reviewer, it is quite possible that you will persistently not see an error that would instantly leap off the page if a different person were reviewing it. A third party might be able to pick up on such errors as:

If you hire me to *ruin* [run] your business, I will do everything to accomplish that goal.

The attached report derails [details] our long-range plan.

We will discuss bonuses after the third curse [course] at dinner.

Correct Grammar

In the eyes of a reader, correct grammar is a strong indicator of the writer's competence. Perfect writing tells the reader that you are well-educated and care about your work. Conversely, poor grammar will lead readers to question whether they should entrust you with responsible tasks. Therefore, here are several areas in which to consider your grammar:

- *Pronouns.* A pronoun is a word that is used instead of a noun or noun phrase, such as "I" or "me." An example of correct usage is "Mary talked to Melissa and *me*." The easy way to discern the correct usage in the preceding sentence is to drop out the other person (Melissa), so that the sentence reads "Mary talked to *me*." Incorrect usage would be "Mary talked to Melissa and *I*."
- *Inverted sentence structures.* In an inverted sentence, the verb comes before the subject. Normally, the reverse is the case. When a sentence begins with "There is," the true subject of the sentence follows the verb, which means that it is an inverted sentence. When this is the case, and the subject is plural, then the associated verb needs to be plural, too. For example, "There *is* many housing options for the refugees" should actually be stated as "There *are* many housing options for the refugees," to bring the verb and noun into alignment.
- *Subject mix.* A sentence might include a mix of subjects, where some are plural and some are singular. Whether the associated verb is singular or plural depends on the *last* of the subjects; thus, if the last listed subject is plural, then so too is the associated verb. For example, "Our field service offerings and a new purple widget *targets* the new market niche." In the preceding example, the plural form of "target" is used, since it links to the last subject listed, which is "widget" in singular form. If the subjects had been reversed, with the plural subject stated last, then the sentence would instead be "Our new purple widget and field service offerings *target* the new market niche."

- *Double negatives*. A double negative is a sentence structure containing two negatives and conveying a negative meaning. A double negative typically involves the word "not" and some other word that has a negative sense. This structure is confusing, and so should be avoided. For example, "I ain't got no time for that" could be restated as "I have no time for that."

- *Starting with a conjunction*. A conjunction is a connector between words, phrases, clauses, or sentences, such as *and*. It is perfectly acceptable to begin a sentence with a conjunction, as long as doing so improves the flow of the narrative. For example, "And furthermore, in the absence of carbon capture technologies, sea levels will rise dramatically." In this example, we are starting with "and" in order to connect a statement made in the preceding sentence with the current sentence.

- *Ending with a preposition*. A preposition is a word governing a noun or pronoun, and expressing a relation to another word in a clause, such as "The man *on* the forklift." Though there is nothing technically wrong with ending a sentence with a preposition, it is frowned upon. For example, the sentence "That is a situation I had not thought *of*" could be better stated as "I had not thought *of* that situation."

- *Irregular verb usage*. An irregular verb is one that does not follow the normal pattern of inflection. For example, the past tense of most verbs simply require an "-ed" ending, such as when "sailed" is the past tense of "sail." An example of an irregular verb is "sing," where the past tense is "sang." Since these verb structures require separate memorization, they are fertile grounds for misstatement. For example, "I *creep* through the tunnel" does not translate to "I *creeped* through the tunnel" in past tense, but rather as "I *crept* through the tunnel."

- *Unclear references*. A sentence may be structured in such a way that the references being made are unclear. For example, "Having been told she was a comprehensive idiot, the supervisor fired her." Who was an idiot, the woman or the supervisor? This situation can be remediated by restructuring the sentence, such as "After she called her supervisor a comprehensive idiot, the supervisor fired her."

- *Watch modifier placement*. Every modifier should be placed next to the word it is modifying, or trouble will ensue. For example, "The manager discussed how to load the dumpster with his employees." It appears that the employees are being loaded into the dumpster. Better wording is "The manager discussed with his employees how to load the dumpster." In the latter case, putting *discussed* and *with* next to each other clarifies the situation.

- *Comma usage*. When in doubt, insert a comma before "and" or "or" when listing three or more items. For example, you can get away with not inserting a comma after the word *oranges* in "apples, oranges and pears" because there are so few items. However, when even more items are listed, it becomes increasingly important to insert commas to delineate each item. Therefore, commas should be inserted before every instance of *and* in the following sentence: "Our goals are to increase revenues in the southern region, build four

distribution warehouses, open 37 new stores, upgrade 83 older stores, and reduce employee turnover by 10%."

- *Apostrophes and plurals*. An apostrophe is the sign ('), which is used to indicate the possessive case, such as "the owner's car." It is almost never acceptable to use an apostrophe to denote the plural form of a word. Thus, more than
one CPA is not described as "CPA's," but rather as "CPAs." This rule does
not apply to lower case letters, or in any situations where its use could prevent
a misunderstanding. For example, saying "the company received all As from
the regulator" looks odd, so use "the company received all A's from the regulator" instead.

- *Comma splices*. A comma splice occurs when independent clauses are linked
by a comma. Each independent clause contains a subject and a verb, so it can
be presented as a separate sentence. In effect, a comma splice combines two
sentences into one long sentence. A better approach is to use a semi-colon or
a coordinating conjunction (such as "and", "but", "or", "so", "for", "nor", and
"yet"). For example, "Incurring a liability triggers an increase in a credit account; paying off a liability triggers a decrease in the same account."

- *Attention getters*. Limit the use of italics and underlining to emphasize a point,
since their frequent use dilutes their impact. Bolding is best limited to headers
and sub-headers. Also, the use of caps for more than a word or two can be
REALLY ANNOYING.

Style Enhancement

In business writing, the main point is to avoid being dull. Picture a reader nodding off
over your document – what are the chances of the person remembering *anything* that
you have written? Here are several tips for avoiding this all-too-common outcome:

- *Engage directly*. Use the pronouns *you* and *your* (or the reader's name) to
engage directly with the reader, rather than the vastly less interesting *I*. For
example, "I conducted a review of inventory record accuracy at the Monroe
Street warehouse on January 4th" sounds much less interesting than "David,
after conducting a review of inventory record accuracy at your Monroe Street
warehouse last Tuesday, we found that your staff had achieved an accuracy
level of 93%."

- *Employ contractions*. Contractions make writing look more informal, which
makes it easier to read. The general rule is that, if you would speak a phrase
using contractions, then do the same in writing. For example, "employees who
do not want to engage in the company's stock purchase plan do not have to"
sounds much stuffier than "If you don't want to buy shares through the company, that's fine with us."

- *Avoid passivity*. Passive writing is all too common in business writing. Avoid
it where possible, since passive writing does not engage the reader in the topic.
An example of passive writing is "inventory counts were conducted by six
count teams until noontime," while a more active approach is "six count teams

conducted inventory counts until noontime." Passive writing is easily identified by the presence of a past-tense verb (such as "conducted" in the last example). Other examples are "the commencement address was deliver*ed* by
Nancy," "the accounting error was discover*ed* by Ellen," and "the collections
team was prais*ed* for their cash collection activities."

- *Vary sentences.* Readers find a document to be more interesting when the sentences structures vary. In particular, introduce a short, choppy sentence into a
paragraph just to break up the monotony. Or, shift a key word or phrase to the
beginning or end of the sentence – whatever has the most impact. For example:

> We have noticed over the past few months that the floating interest rate
> linked to our line of credit has been trending upward. How is this possible?
> Because the Fed has increased the federal funds rate twice in the last three
> months. Can we expect more of this? Yes, as long as the inflation rate con-
> tinues to increase.

In the preceding example, the number of words in each sentence were 23, then
four, then 15, then six, and then 10. The outcome is a conversational style that
is easy to read.

- *Minimize acronyms.* It is much easier to write using acronyms, since they
compress the writing task. For example, KPI is easier to write than "key performance indicator." However, if the reader does not understand an acronym,
then he may end up scanning through the document for the full text, which
breaks up her reading flow. In those cases in which you still want to include
an acronym in the text, at least place the acronym next to the full text in pa-
rentheses, so that the reader can see the translation. For example:

> A key performance indicator (KPI) is a core metric used by a business to
> monitor its progress toward achieving key goals and financial outcomes.

- *Avoid formality.* An excessive level of formality in a document appears pompous and stiff. For example, "subsequent to our conversation on Tuesday"
could be replaced by "after we talked last Tuesday." In short, write the way
you would speak.
- *Adopt a pleasant tone.* How many times have we read an angry missive and
immediately discounted its contents just because of the tone? Certainly, the
writer might have been justified in being annoyed, but letting this emotion
leak through onto the written page was a mistake. Using words like "delu-
sional" or "deranged" have no place in business writing. A better approach is
to appear relaxed and likeable, thereby rendering the tone of the document a
nonevent. That being said, your tone can vary, depending on the recipient. A
more informal approach is certainly allowable when you know the person
well, while a more formal structure might be called for when there is no relationship at all. For example, a message to a good friend might begin with

"Dear Andrea," while a message to a new sales prospect might begin with "Dear Ms. Folsom."

Tip: When a word sounds too negative, look for a synonym that is not so adverse. For example, replace *not important* with *minor*.

- *Sprinkle in some humor.* Business is a serious business (ahem), but the related writing can be so stodgy that a hint of mirth can improve the acceptance of your documents. However, humor can be radioactive when targeted at the wrong person, so be careful to keep your puns and jokes well within the acceptable boundaries. It is more difficult to insert humor into writing, since you cannot see the reader's reaction, so this is a case in which an exceedingly careful touch is advisable. That being said, humorous writing can take the edge off a situation in which there has been a major screw-up, such as the following:

  > To: All those declared dead by our payroll system

  > If you did not receive a paycheck this morning, it is because the computer confused our "D" deduction code for dental insurance with being deceased. I was also declared deceased, so I suppose this memo is taking the form of a séance. We are hastening to correct the situation, should have manual checks prepared by midafternoon, and will deliver them to you as soon as they are ready.

  Humor is also useful when asking people to do something that they really don't want to do, such as work overtime. Here is an example:

  > The good news is that we got the Mickelson account, and the bad news is the same thing. I'm afraid they want ad copy by next Thursday evening at the latest – which is right before the holiday on Friday. Yep, I know, I'm an idiot. If it will make you feel any better, I will be available with whipped cream and pie plates all day on Thursday, in case you want to give me a face-full.

- *Avoid sarcasm.* Since sarcasm involves the use of cutting remarks, it naturally follows that it has no place in business writing (note the previous comments regarding adopting a pleasant tone). Further, it annoys the recipient, who will be less inclined to deal with you in the future.

Tip: Include anything you want in the first draft, since it doesn't have to be perfect on the first pass. Just be sure to take out what doesn't seem appropriate during the review process.

Read Great Writers

One of the best ways to improve your writing is to copy the styles of great writers. Reading through their works slowly and making note of their word choice, sentence structure, punctuation, paragraphing, and arguments is an excellent way to gain knowledge about how to improve your writing. Some of the better business writers worth reading are Gary Hamel, Eliyahu Goldratt, and C.K. Prahalad. The same approach can be used with any great writer; consider reading the works of the winners of the Nobel prize in literature, the Booker prize, and the National Book Award.

The same approach can be applied to business publications, since their writing is more directly applicable to your needs. For example, read through the British magazine *The Economist* to see how its writers convey basic economic principles and issues within relatively short articles.

A Word on Overpolishing

Engaging in a detailed writing process does not mean that you should spend inordinate amounts of time going over (and over, and over) a document. This document is so overpolished that it gleams in the moonlight. At some point, every document needs to be released into the wild, so that people can actually read it. Otherwise, there is a distinctly unfavorable cost-benefit analysis associated with everything you write, because you are spending too much time on them. This is a particular problem with people who are dreadfully concerned about issuing something that does not have precisely the right tone, or which does not take into account every possible feeling of the recipient. Ultimately, these people are driven by the fear that they will get it wrong.

One way to deal with this mindset is to consistently follow the same writing process every time, which involves a certain maximum number of iterations at each step. Once the maximum number of iterations has been met (such as two re-reads) then shut down the project and issue the document. This approach does not yield a guaranteed 100% level of perfection, but what you release should get the job done.

The Flesch Reading Ease Readability Formula

The Flesch Reading Ease formula is a useful tool for quantifying the readability of text. It was developed by Rudolph Flesch, a writing consultant, in 1948. The formula is:

$$\text{Readability ease} = 206.835 - (1.015 \times \text{ASL}) - (84.6 \times \text{ASW})$$

Where:

ASL =   Average sentence length, which is the number of words divided by the number of sentences

ASW =   Average number of syllables per word, which is the number of syllables divided by the number of words

The output of this formula is a number that can range from zero to 100. A higher number indicates that text is easier to read. A score between 90 and 100 is considered easily understandable by a 5th grade student, while a score between 60 and 70 should be easily understood by an 8th or 9th grade student. A score between zero and 30 should be easily understood by a college student. The following exhibit shows the ease of readability for various ranges of scores.

Readability Score Range

Score Range	Ease of Readability
90-100	Very easy
80-89	Easy
70-79	Fairly easy
60-69	Standard
50-59	Fairly difficult
30-49	Difficult
0-29	Very confusing

By working with the reading ease formula, you can convert dense writing into something more understandable, simply by continually revising the text in order to drive up the score. For example, we present two versions of the same company mission statement, with the second one having been tightened up to give it a better readability score. The initial version is:

> The company exists to provide leading-edge thought leaders the opportunity to discuss their cogitations on advanced issues relating to the future direction of the human race, including insights into global warming, race relations, warfare in third-world countries, and environmental pollution concerns. By doing so, we hope to foster advancements in the well-being of people around the world.

The tightened version is:

> Spread ideas.

The second version is the actual mission statement of TED, which sponsors talks by leading individuals around the world. The readability score for our initial (and quite florid) version of TED's mission statement is 28, while the readability score of the improved version is 78.

Writing Emails

When writing emails, remember that you are trying to get your message to stand out from the massive flood of messages being received by the targeted person. Therefore, if you do not design the email to stand out from the crowd, it will barely register with the recipient, if the person even bothers to read the message. To improve your odds of having the recipient actually read your email, consider making the following adjustments to your email writing:

- *Upgrade the subject line*. Make your request easy to find among the incoming flood of messages. For example, "A Request" subject line is less likely to be opened than "Need Money to Upgrade Server Room."
- *Get to the point*. Don't waste time. State your message within the first couple of sentences. Anything longer, and the recipient will click on the delete button. If you persist in issuing multi-page treatises by email, you will come across as a pompous blowhard.
- *Minimize copying*. Do not spray your emails amongst a large number of people, since you are merely clogging their in boxes, which is annoying. Instead, only copy to people who can actually use the information. Also, use the reply all feature sparingly, since it expands the amount of email flooding.
- *Adhere to the conventions*. Even when creating an email on a phone, always use standard capitalization and punctuation. This takes extra time, but it keeps readers from thinking that you are a careless writer. This is a particular concern when emailing from a phone, since the autocorrect function can result in some hysterically incorrect messages that will take extra time to explain to readers.

The following exhibit contains two versions of an email, where the first version ignores the email conventions noted here, and the second adheres to them. Perhaps you can see a difference.

Two Variations on an Email

Message Ignoring Email Conventions	Message Adhering to Email Conventions
Subject: More problems	Subject: Request for Backup Generator
Hi Dave,	Dave,
Remember the server problems we had last month? They were caused by a short in the power systems after a tree branch fell on the power line running into our building. That event burned out 14 servers, our main laser printer, and four monitors. Not to mention shutting down the order entry system for two days, AND the accounting system, AND the warehouse system, AND the purchasing software. Because of these many issues, I have attached a proposal for a backup generator and power filtering system that should keep these problems from occurring again in the future. I know we don't have this funding in the budget, but the same problem could come up again at any time, so I'm requesting special funding for the purchase and installation.	To keep from suffering from last month's massive computer failures a second time, I'm attaching a proposal for a backup generator and power filtering system. There is no funding in the budget for this, so can you please talk to the president on our behalf? You know him better than I do! Many thanks, Bob, IT Manager
Thanks! Bob	

The essential difference between the two emails is brevity. The second version requires fewer than half the number of words, and gets straight to the point – the IT manager needs money right now to fix a serious problem, and is asking for help.

Personnel issues should mostly be handled in person. However, when it is not possible to issue a reprimand in person, it may be necessary to use email. When this is the case, the email needs to be as factual as possible, stating the infraction, why it was wrong, and the potential consequences. The following sample email illustrates how a reprimand should be handled:

Subject: Malware Attached to Your Email

Francis,

Yesterday, you sent an email entitled "Hilarious Animal Stunts" to everyone in the sales department, sending it from your home computer. That email contained a link to a malware download, which 14 people clicked on to access what they thought was your video. As a result, the data on those 14 computers have been encrypted and are not recoverable. Our company policy clearly states that intra-company emails are only to be sent from company computers, for this very reason. What you have done is a clear breach of company policy, which has caused significant harm to the business. This matter is so severe that I am referring it to HR, who will be contacting you shortly regarding further actions.

Anna

The tone of the preceding reprimand is severe, because it has to be; the employee has caused major damage to the business. Nonetheless, it avoids outright anger, sticking to the facts of the situation and pointing out what will happen next.

Emails are usually written and sent very quickly, which introduces two problems; they are more likely to contain typos, and they may contain a tone that is offensive to the recipient. These are especially critical issues when you consider that they can be forwarded on to a third party within moments, so that your gaffes could be distributed to a large audience. Given these risks, it makes a great deal of sense to thoroughly review each e-mail before pressing the send button. Also, consider letting the more sensitive emails sit for an hour or so before sending them, just to make sure that the tone you are conveying is really such a good idea. After all, emails can be easily misconstrued.

It is too easy to convey bad news via email, when it really should be conveyed in person. Therefore, do not treat email as a metaphorical shield for the more difficult communications. Instead, go forth and talk to the other party in person. It may not be pleasant, but direct speech is sometimes the only way to discuss something with another party.

Writing Social Media Posts

Social media posts are frequently written from a smart phone, which brings up the problem of typos. Even the best auto-fill software is unable to create a perfectly-worded post. Instead, all too many posts are laced with errors. This may not be an issue when social media is employed just for personal use, but that is not the case at all when it is used in business. In the latter case, it is essential to edit before releasing a post. Otherwise, a plethora of errors could damage your reputation with business associates.

Writing Blog Posts

A blog is a regularly-updated web page that is written in an informal or conversational style. Many businesses maintain a blog, so that they can communicate more directly with their customers. Blog posts can be used to present current issues and opportunities being faced by the company, and can serve to develop a sense of community among customers. Blog entries are typically written in a conversational style, such as:

> We've just released the new purple widget, and it even comes in a left-handed style! If you want to check it out, we will have a few demo units available during an informal rollout at The Irish Embassy Pub this Tuesday night, from 6 to 8 p.m.

Blog postings are intended to be short. Readers expect to scan through a post quickly to the essential information, so assist them by using bold and italics to highlight key points. If there are more than a few points, organize them into bullet points to enhance readability. Also, connect blog postings to other information on the company website (or elsewhere) with hyperlinks, to increase their usefulness to readers.

Note: A blog is considered an official company function, so make sure that all posts are edited before being posted to ensure that they adhere to official company policy and ethical standards.

Writing Complaint Letters

A complaint letter describes a problem that you want to have rectified. Writing a complaint letter can be a delicate task, especially when you are boiling with fury at the presumed idiocy of the other party. Though it may feel good to do so, a scathing letter does little to convince the recipient to take action. A better approach is to describe the problem as rationally as possible, note the steps you have taken to rectify matters, and ask for assistance. Therefore, the basic structure of a complaint letter should be:

1. Identify the problem and supply all necessary supporting information.
2. Explain what went wrong as clearly as possible.
3. Specify what you want the recipient to do about it.

A sample complaint letter that follows this structure is:

On November 8, I called your customer service department and ordered 500 pairs of safety glasses in various sizes. The order number was 843901A. On November 14, I received a pallet of 100 safety helmets, for which the attached order number was 834901A. It appears that your shipping department transposed the second and third digits in the order number, so that I received helmets instead of safety glasses. I immediately rejected the order, sending the helmets back to your company. Since then, I have been billed for the helmets, and have not received the safety glasses.

I have enclosed copies of all pertinent information. If you cannot send me the safety glasses by November 20, please cancel the order.

Responding to Complaint Letters

Letter-writing can be particularly difficult when responding to a customer complaint. It is never a good idea to strike back at the customer, since doing so will probably lose the customer, and the letter could also end up on social media, causing major damage to the company's reputation. The following exhibit contains side-by-side examples of a business letter, where the first version illustrates what not to do, and the second version shows a more customer-friendly face.

Two Variations on Responses to a Customer Complaint

Letter Abusing the Customer	Letter Taking a More Conciliatory Tone
I am startled that you thought our consulting work was inadequate. We warned you at the start of the engagement that the software would require numerous changes to your existing procedures, and yet you refused to change them and instead required numerous software alterations that pushed back the completion date by nine months and called for more than 2,000 hours of additional testing work. It is a miracle that we managed to deliver the product at all! Given your intransigence, any impartial observer would have to conclude that we performed incredibly well.	I agree that the delivery date was well past your initial expectation. But we believed that we should extend the timeline in order to accommodate your requests, to ensure that you ultimately received a system that satisfied your needs. It does appear that the system now works quite well for you; your customer service manager recently mentioned to me that her department is at least one-third more efficient than before the system was installed. So, I think it was a trade-off of swapping more time for a system that works better for you.

In the preceding example, we have gone from a combative tone to one that focuses instead on the trade-off between a delayed delivery date and a better product.

Writing Adjustment Letters

An adjustment letter is a message written in response to a complaint, telling your customer what you plan to do about the issue. Though an adjustment letter is sent in response to a specific problem, it provides a great opportunity to build goodwill for the business. When structured properly, an adjustment letter goes beyond damage repair, to restore customer confidence in the company. A critical part of any adjustment letter is its tone, which should be positive and respectful. Immediately take responsibility for the problem, and then shift to what you are doing to correct it. For example:

Dear Ms. Swindon:

We are sorry about the end of your vacation with us, when our staff accidentally dropped your suitcase into the ocean while transferring it from a boat to the dock, destroying your laptop computer. We are eager to restore your confidence in our resort, so please accept the enclosed $3,000 check to assist in your purchase of a replacement laptop. Also, should you choose to stay with us again, we will upgrade you to the master's cabin on the boat, free of charge.

This incident highlighted a problem with our baggage handling procedures, which we are correcting at once. We are using this incident as a training case for our staff, to ensure that it never happens again. Further, we are installing a concrete lip on the edge of the dock, to keep luggage from rolling off. Again, I am so sorry for the loss of your computer.

Here is another adjustment letter that follows the same principles:

Dear Mr. Hart,

We are deeply sorry about our dry-cleaning mistake that ruined your suit. In compensation, I have enclosed a check for $1,500 to pay for a new one. In addition, we have altered our operating procedures to ensure that the staff correctly identifies silk suits, which call for a different cleaning process than the one applied to your suit. I hope that you will forgive our mistake and continue to use the Kingsman Dry Cleaning Service for your future dry-cleaning needs. Thank you.

There may be cases in which only a partial adjustment is being made, because the customer may be (at least partially) at fault. In this case, the intent is mainly to regain the lost goodwill of the customer, while providing instruction on how to use the company's product correctly. When writing this type of adjustment letter, remember that the customer believes his claim to be justified, so give an explanation for the product failure right away, and then talk about the claim. For example:

Dear Ms. Mercado:

Enclosed is your game controller, which you shipped to us on September 15.

Our repair staff reports that the controller was damaged by your dog having chewed on it, as evidenced by the tooth marks on the casing. Also, it appears that your dog's drool then penetrated the casing and destroyed the controller board. As noted in the instruction manual on page 17, the controller can be damaged by excessive jostling.

We have replaced the controller board, reassembled the unit, and tested it to ensure that it is working properly. To avoid similar problems in the future, I suggest storing the game controller on a high shelf when it is not in use.

If you experience this problem again, please call us at 800-888-1234 to discuss alternative solutions.

Note: Both of the adjustment letters in this section refer to actual events, and accurately reflect how they were handled.

Writing Business Letters

While emails account for the bulk of all business writing, there is still a need for actual business letters, covering matters as diverse as dunning letters to customers, announcing the initiation of a new service, and contacting the government about a tax dispute. When writing a letter, the first concern is its layout. The following exhibit contains the basic structure of a business letter, extending from the letterhead block down through the end notations.

Basic Structure of a Business Letter

Letterhead	142 E. Front Street Butte, MT 59701 [Company Logo] Phone 406-987-4321
Date	January 10, 20X3
Address	Ms. Carol Standage Vice President of Operations Denver Railcar Maintenance Corp. 43 Wynkoop Street Denver, CO 80202
Salutation	Dear Ms. Standage:
Body	Thank you for spending time with us last week to tour your facilities and gain a greater understanding of your railcar maintenance out-sourcing needs. I believe we can provide you with a competitive solution that will result in 20% faster maintenance turnaround time, as well as 8% lower costs. I have enclosed our proposal that describes the details of what we can do for you.
Complimentary closing	Sincerely,
Signature	*Ernest Henderson*
Signature block	Ernest Henderson President Butte Rail Services, Inc.
End notations	Enclosure: Maintenance outsourcing proposal

When written properly, a business letter can advance the interests of a business by convincing the recipient to act in the manner you want, such as by paying an overdue invoice or buying a company product. Use the following points to write better business letters:

- *Focus on them.* Write the letter to appeal to the interests of the recipient, rather than you. This means sprinkling the letter with the words *you* and *your*, and avoiding the word *I*, since the focus is on them, not you.
- *Get to the point.* As is the case in all business writing, get to the point – right away. Wasting the reader's time with such platitudes as "I hope this message

finds you well" runs the risk of the person throwing the letter away, and makes it more difficult for the recipient to dig deeper and find the real point of the message.

- *Set the tone.* Even if the letter recipient is a well-known grouch, this does not mean that you have to write in the same tone. Instead, be polite and reasonable throughout your letter. Doing so is professional, and gives the other person less reason to be annoyed, even if the letter conveys bad news.
- *Don't waffle.* When there is bad news to deliver, many people waffle on transmitting it, such as "we do not have a position for you at this time, but encourage you to contact us periodically to inquire about other positions." No. This approach even encourages the recipient to keep badgering the company, which is not a desirable outcome. Instead, state the message and get on with life, such as "sorry, but the position for which you applied has been filled."
- *Eliminate stock phrases.* Business letters are cluttered with stock phrases, such as "enclosed herein" and "we are in receipt of." These phrases unnecessarily expand the size of the letter and detract from its readability. Instead, use wording such as "enclosed are" and "we've received."

The following side-by-side examples of a business letter illustrate some of these concepts.

Two Variations on a Business Letter

Letter Ignoring Business Conventions	Letter Adhering to Business Conventions
Dear Sir/Madam:	Dear Henry:
The Himalayan Climbers Association (HCA) of Kathmandu is pleased to be in receipt of your annual membership fee. Doing so helps HCA towards it goal of having 10,000 members by the end of this year. Buying this membership offers up a world of opportunities, including networking with fellow members, beer bashes in the HCA's downtown headquarters in Kathmandu, and discounts on climbing equipment with several select outfitters.	We are so pleased to have you as a new member of the Himalayan Climbers Association! We can assist you with networking possibilities, beer bashes in our downtown headquarters, and discounts with local climbing retailers. Please call us if you require any specialized concierge services.
Yours truly, The Himalayan Climbers Association	Sincerely, Paul Irvine, HCA President

In the preceding exhibit, the first letter initially focuses on the organization, rather than the customer, does not get to the point until the second half of the letter, uses the passive voice, and incorporates a stock phrase, "pleased to be in receipt of." The second letter avoids these issues and, as is frequently the case with better writing, is also shorter than the first letter.

The following text could be used as part of a letter that conveys bad news to the recipient, and makes use of the first three bullet points pertaining to writing business letters:

Dear Amelia,

Thank you for your order of our new Electrolight airplane. You have chosen the world's first all-electric commuter plane for your fleet, and I am sure you will find that the elimination of fuel costs and greatly reduced servicing costs will greatly improve your profitability.

Unfortunately, we have encountered some delays in the flight certification process with the Federal Aviation Administration that will delay the release date of the plane until November. However, be assured that your order is at the top of our priority list, and we will expedite production of the 10 planes as soon as the FAA issues an airworthiness certificate.

Would you be interested in coming out to watch the FAA's test flights? They will have a review team here all of next week, and we would be delighted to have you watch the proceedings. Please call me if I can be of assistance in any way.

Fred Noonan, Electrolight President

In the preceding bad news letter, notice how the negative point (delayed product delivery) is sandwiched between a couple of "happy thought" items, to lessen the blow of the bad news. Also, the focus of the letter is entirely on the customer, and the writer keeps the tone relatively optimistic. The recipient may not be too happy about the late delivery, but at least the manner in which the news was couched cannot cause her any additional grief.

A particular annoyance for readers is when a letter grants a request, but only grudgingly. As a result, the business gains no points with the reader from granting the request – rather the reverse – and probably gains a reputation for being bureaucratic, too. Here is an example:

Hi Sally, I received your request to expedite the $100,000 purchase of a replacement MegaVax system to replace the one that broke last week. As you know, company policy mandates that purchases of this size be approved in advance by the vice president of manufacturing, the CFO, the president, and the board of directors, which normally takes about three months. However, given your insistence on the matter, and calls to the president's home last weekend, he has authorized an immediate purchase. I will have Purchasing send you a purchase order this afternoon. In the future, please go through the normal channels when requesting purchases.

A more moderate tone would have been a bit less petulant, such as:

Hi Sally, this MegaVax replacement must be important to you! The president called me right after you called him last Saturday, and told me to get after it. I walked it through Purchasing this morning, so you should have the purchase order this afternoon. Best of luck with the install! Perhaps we can chat about the process over lunch some time?

Writing Memos

A memo is a brief written message or report. It is typically issued within a business, and is intended to either inform others about a specific topic or encourage action. Given the specific uses to which memos are put, they should be written in the following way:

1. *Title*. Select a title that states the precise nature of the memo. Several examples of good memo headers are "Flaws Found in Parking Garage Structure," "Pricing for Jones Proposal," and "Results of Research on Fires in Routt County." Each of these examples tells you the exact contents of the memo. The same concept can be applied to sub-headers, such as "10 Ways to Cut Costs" or "Problems Found During Customer Visits."

2. *Key points*. State each issue, the proposed solution, and the reasons for that solution. For example:

   > Issue: Micron Metallic has been consistently late in delivering components for our washing machines. In the past month, its deliveries averaged five business days late.
   >
   > Proposed Solution: Reduce Micron to a secondary supplier, and promote MetalCraft Industries to be the main supplier of these components.
   >
   > Supporting Comments: MetalCraft is located only eight miles away from the company, and so is in a good position to make timely deliveries. They have also delivered on time in nine out of ten test orders. Making this switch allows us to clear out a backlog of work-in-process, which reduces our working capital requirements, while also being able to make deliveries to our customers with a shorter lead time.

This succinct approach puts every key issue in front of the reader, stating the main argument and then providing supporting details.

Whenever a memo is presenting an argument for a course of action, assume that it will be picked apart by those with an opposing position. When this is the case, have one or more people who are conversant in the subject matter review the memo. They can provide critical analyses about how well your presented arguments hold up. It is better to deal with these concerns before the memo is formally released to the target audience, since doing so will improve the odds of success.

When writing memos, writers have a tendency to run over – sometimes *way* over. The problem is that their initial topic turns out to be larger than expected, so that they uncover too many points to be covered within a few pages. The result can have the same length as a doctoral dissertation. This problem can be dealt with by defining the topic as tightly as possible, until only a couple of points are left. If it does appear possible to pare down the topic this much, then initially issue a memo dealing with the core issue(s) and then keep releasing additional memos covering ancillary topics until the recipients are satisfied. This approach usually results in less work, and allows for at least some topics to be addressed fairly quickly.

Writing Press Releases

A press release is a brief statement about a company event that is released for outside consumption. Press releases can be used to issue many kinds of information that may be of interest to the public, such as:

- New hires into senior management, along with their resumes. Investors can use this information to estimate the impact of a new hire on a company's operations.
- The receipt of a contract award, along with the amount of associated revenue and the period over which the revenue is to be earned. Investors can incorporate this information into their valuation models for the business.
- New facility openings, which is of particular importance when the facility is a new store location. Investors can then estimate the likely revenue to be generated by the new location.
- New product launches, including enough specifics for investors to estimate likely revenue levels that will result, and the extent to which the new product sales may cannibalize the sales of existing products.

In a press release, the event being described is placed within the first one or two sentences, followed by a management statement about the event, followed by general information about the company. This level of brevity is needed to reduce the distribution cost of a press release, which is typically priced by word count. A sample press release is:

Date   **FOR IMMEDIATE RELEASE**

Hegemony Awarded Gaming Contract

Boston, Massachusetts – Hegemony Toy Company has been awarded a contract by the U.S. Naval War College to develop a gaming platform that can be used to train members of the U.S. Navy and other members of NATO in how to deal with open ocean threat situations. The contract is for $5 million, and is to be completed within 24 months.

"Hegemony is bringing its expertise in developing military-oriented games to the professional military," states Hegemony president Douglas Bradley. "We will use our Nelson seaborne gaming software to provide a unique solution for the War College. This patented system is uniquely designed for the multi-player distributed environment that the War College envisions for this critical tool."

About Hegemony Toy Company

Hegemony is a provider of military-oriented toys and games to the under-20 age group. Its primary offerings are in the areas of board games and multi-player on-line games.

Contact Information

Gerry Patton
123 Bastogne Way
Boston, Massachusetts 02203
Phone: 617-330-8900
E-mail: _____

In the sample press release, the event summarization states the name of the customer, the amount of revenue expected, and the time period over which the revenue is to be earned. The public can use this information to alter their estimates of company financial performance. In addition, the press release points out the existence and use of intellectual property, which improves investor perceptions of the company's intangible assets.

Additional examples of the primary content of a press release are:

(1) Hegemony Toy Company has just licensed its Napoleon Wars board game to a distributor in the United Kingdom. As a result of this agreement, Hegemony expects to build recognition for its other products in its target age group in the United Kingdom market.

(2) Hegemony Toy Company has just hired Mr. Dale Trotsky as its vice president of manufacturing. Mr. Trotsky has deep experience in lean manufacturing practices, which Hegemony expects him to use to drive down costs within the Hegemony manufacturing facilities.

(3) Hegemony Toy Company has just released its new Thirty Years War multi-player online gaming platform. The game is available to users worldwide, and is paid for with a $15 per month subscription fee.

In the first example, the press release is used to announce a potential increase in the company's target market. In the second example, the press release tells investors that the company intends to reduce costs through the revision of its manufacturing practices. The third example reveals that the company intends to create a recurring revenue stream with a subscription-based sales model. Thus, each press release conveys a specific message that the public would likely consider to be valuable.

Where possible, quantify the information conveyed in a press release. A greater level of detail is more useful to readers, since they can use it to more accurately estimate the timing and amount of a company's earnings. Examples of the requisite level of detail are:

(1) The contract has maximum funding of $5 million. The customer has the option to extend the contract for an additional five years, with maximum funding of $3 million in each of the additional years.

(2) The outsourcing agreement provides that the company will pay the supplier $15 million per year for the next ten years for outsourced IT services, with a built-in inflation adjustment that is capped at 5% per year.

(3) The company recognized a charge of $25 million associated with the facility shutdown for employee terminations and environmental remediation. These payments should be completed within the next six months.

It is most efficient to distribute press releases through a press release distribution service. Their in-house proofreaders examine every press release prior to distribution, which can result in minor improvements to the presentation and content of a release.

Summary

The amount of work described in this book to create well-crafted text might seem like overkill, especially when you are overwhelmed with work already. However, every written communication you issue is a commentary on your skill and commitment to the job. Even a simple writing gaffe could ruin a presentation, an otherwise persuasive research paper, or a presentation to a client. Therefore, it is always worthwhile to go through a standardized writing process to initially create a document, and then another standardized review process to polish it. Just remember: Good writing is good business.

Glossary

A

Apostrophe. The sign ('), which is used to indicate the possessive case, such as "the owner's car."

B

Blog. A regularly-updated web page that is written in an informal or conversational style.

C

Cliché. A phrase that is overused and betrays a lack of original thought.

Conjunction. A connector between words, phrases, clauses, or sentences, such as *and* or *but*.

D

Double negative. A sentence structure containing two negatives and conveying a negative meaning.

I

Inverted sentence. A sentence in which the verb comes before the subject.

Irregular verb. A verb that does not follow the normal pattern of inflection.

J

Jargon. Special words or phrases that are used within a profession or industry, and which are difficult for others to understand.

M

Memo. A brief written message or report.

P

Paragraph. A distinct section of a piece of writing, usually dealing with a single theme and indicated by a new indentation or line.

Preposition. A word governing and usually preceding a noun or pronoun, and expressing a relation to another word, such as *at, on, with, over*, and *under*.

Press release. A brief statement about a company event that is released for outside consumption.

Pronoun. A word that is used instead of a noun or noun phrase.

W

Writer's block. The condition of being unable to think of what to write or how to proceed with writing.

Index

www.ingramcontent.com/pod-product-compliance
Lightning Source LLC
Chambersburg PA
CBHW051425200326
41520CB00023B/7358